Mary Fields

CHERRY LAKE PRESS

Published in the United States of America by Cherry Lake Publishing Group
Ann Arbor, Michigan
www.cherrylakepublishing.com

Reading Adviser: Beth Walker Gambro, MS, Ed., Reading Consultant, Yorkville, IL
Book Designer: Jennifer Wahi
Illustrator: Jeff Bane

Photo Credits: page 5: © KennStilger47/Shutterstock; page 7: Courtesy of Tennessee State Library & Archives, Tennessee Postcard Collection; pages 9, 22: Courtesy of Toledo Lucas County Public Library; pages 11, 23: Smithsonian, National Postal Museum; pages 13, 15, 17, 19: Courtesy of Wedsworth Memorial Library, Cascade, Montana;
page 21: Montana Historical Society

Cherry Lake Press is an imprint of Cherry Lake Publishing Group.

Library of Congress Cataloging-in-Publication Data has been filed and is available at catalog.loc.gov.

Printed in the United States of America
Corporate Graphics

About the author: Kelisa Wing loves spending time with her family and loves helping others. She lives in northern Virginia.

About the illustrator: Jeff Bane and his two business partners own a studio along the American River in Folsom, California, home of the 1849 Gold Rush. When Jeff's not sketching or illustrating for clients, he's either swimming or kayaking in the river to relax.

I was born **enslaved** around 1832 in Tennessee. I was freed in my early 30s.

I found work on steamboats.
I traveled around the United
States.

I moved to Ohio. I worked for **nuns** at a **convent** there. I was the **groundskeeper**.

Where have you lived?

I later moved to Montana. I had a **reputation** for being tough. This helped me get a job as a **Star Route Carrier**.

How would you describe yourself?

I was the first Black woman to do this job. I was nicknamed Stagecoach Mary.

I delivered mail for 8 years.
I protected mail from thieves.

What do you like to do?

I lived in the town of Cascade.
I grew a garden.

I **retired** from delivering the mail.
I opened my own laundry business.

My legacy continues. In Montana, they made my birthday a holiday.

What would you like to ask me?

1870

1830

Born
1832

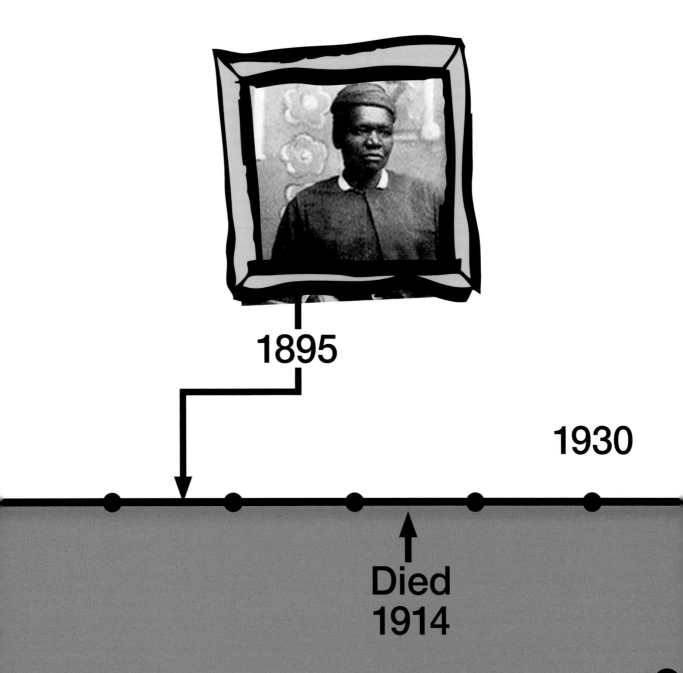

1895

1930

Died
1914

glossary

convent (KAHN-vent) a place where a group of nuns live

enslaved (en-SLAYVD) made a slave, held in slavery or bondage

groundskeeper (GROWNDZ-kee-puhr) person who takes care of the grounds of a large property

nuns (NUHNZ) women who belong to a religious community and devote their life to God

reputation (reh-pyuh-TAY-shuhn) overall character as judged by people

retired (rih-TYRD) not working

Star Route Carrier (STAHR ROOT KEHR-ee-uhr) a private mail carrier who takes mail from the post office or railroad station to another post office

index